## Learning to Read, Step by Step!

**Ready to Read**   **Preschool–Kindergarten**
• big type and easy words • rhyme and rhythm • picture clues
For children who know the alphabet and are eager to begin reading.

**Reading with Help**   **Preschool–Grade 1**
• basic vocabulary • short sentences • simple stories
For children who recognize familiar words and sound out new words with help.

**Reading on Your Own**   **Grades 1–3**
• engaging characters • easy-to-follow plots • popular topics
For children who are ready to read on their own.

**Reading Paragraphs**   **Grades 2–3**
• challenging vocabulary • short paragraphs • exciting stories
For newly independent readers who read simple sentences with confidence.

**Ready for Chapters**   **Grades 2–4**
• chapters • longer paragraphs • full-color art
For children who want to take the plunge into chapter books but still like colorful pictures.

**STEP INTO READING®** is designed to give every child a successful reading experience. The grade levels are only guides; children will progress through the steps at their own speed, developing confidence in their reading. The F&P Text Level on the back cover serves as another tool to help you choose the right book for your child.

Remember, a lifetime love of reading starts with a single step!

*For Sissy —S.B.*

*To my gorgeous children Henry and Charlotte —P.B.*

Text copyright © 2008 by Samantha Brooke
Cover art and interior illustrations copyright © 2008 by Peter Bull Art Studio

All rights reserved. Published in the United States by Random House Children's Books, a division of Penguin Random House LLC, New York. Originally published in trade paperback in the United States by Penguin Young Readers, an imprint of Penguin Random House LLC, New York, in 2008.

Step into Reading, Random House, and the Random House colophon are registered trademarks of Penguin Random House LLC.

Visit us on the Web!
StepIntoReading.com
rhcbooks.com

Educators and librarians, for a variety of teaching tools, visit us at
RHTeachersLibrarians.com

Library of Congress Cataloging-in-Publication Data is available upon request.
ISBN 978-0-593-43248-8 (trade) — ISBN 978-0-593-43249-5 (lib. bdg.)

Printed in the United States of America
10 9 8 7 6 5 4 3 2 1

This book has been officially leveled by using the F&P Text Level Gradient™ Leveling System.

# Coral Reefs
## in Danger

by Samantha Brooke
illustrated by Peter Bull

Random House 🏠 New York

It is morning. The sun rises over the ocean. Something is poking out of the water. It looks like a tree branch. But it is not a tree branch.

It is coral. Below the
waves is a busy world—the
world of a coral reef.

A coral reef is home to many creatures. Thousands of different small fish live here. So do sharks, eels, and octopuses. Whales and sea turtles also come to visit.

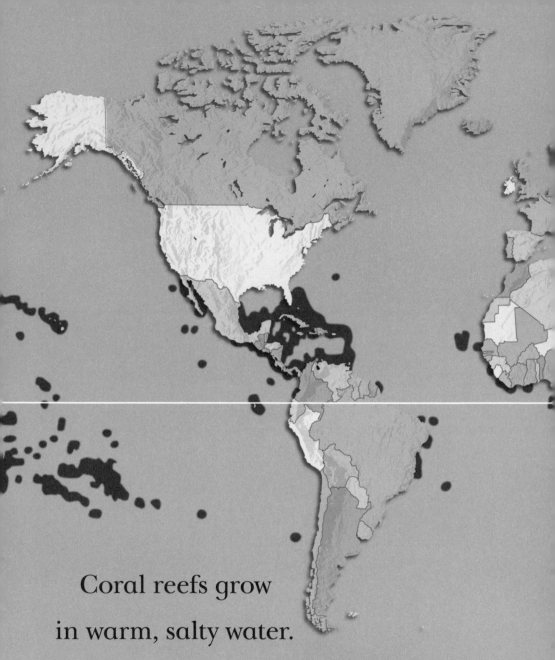

Coral reefs grow
in warm, salty water.

On this map, coral reefs are in red.

Most are near the equator in shallow

water.

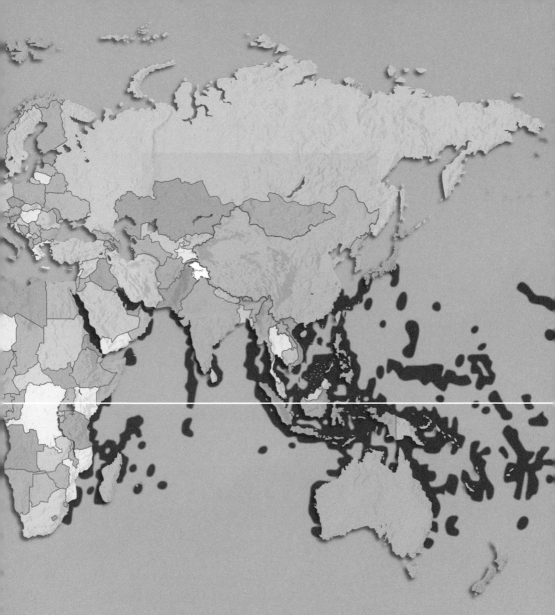

That's because a coral reef needs
lots of sunlight. Deep water is too
dark and cold for most forms
of coral.

Great Barrier Reef

Australia

The largest reef is off the coast of Australia. The Great Barrier Reef stretches for over 1,250 miles. Astronauts can see it from space!

But if coral isn't a rock, what exactly is it? Coral is an animal. The hard outside is the skeleton. Inside is the animal.

Lobsters and crabs also have skeletons on the outside.

A coral reef starts with one small polyp (say: POL-up). It attaches itself to a rock.

The polyp is shaped like a tube. Its mouth is at the top. Around the mouth are tiny tentacles that help catch food.

Over and over again a polyp sprouts new polyps. It is like a tree with new branches.

Coral grows very slowly. And it always stays in the same place.

A group of the same polyps is called a colony.

A colony can grow to be as big as
a house. It can live for hundreds of
years.

Not all coral colonies look the same.

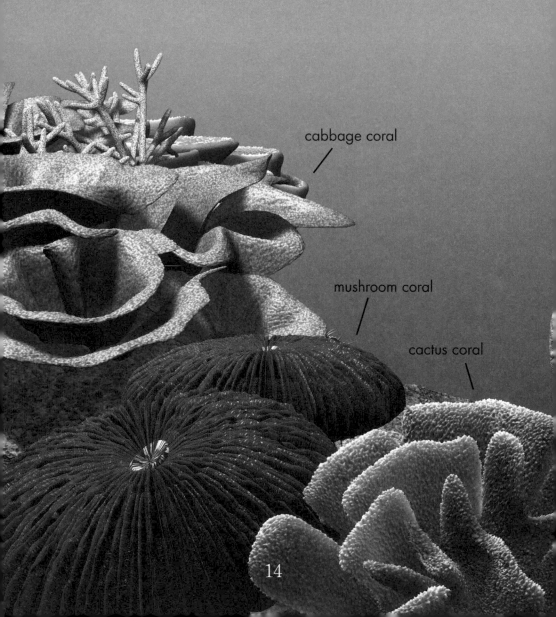

cabbage coral

mushroom coral

cactus coral

Staghorn coral looks like deer antlers. Mushroom coral looks like the underside of a mushroom.

finger coral

brain coral

Daytime is the best time to visit a coral reef. That's when colorful fish are out and about.

There are thousands of different fish in a reef.

At night, colorful fish are in
danger. Sharks, eels, rays,
and octopuses come
hunting for food.

Many fish hide deep in the reef.
Others swim to deeper water. That
doesn't stop sharks from hunting.

Sharks use their sense of smell to
find food. But this white-tipped reef
shark swims right by a parrot fish.

Why? The parrot fish has wrapped
itself in a sticky bubble. The shark
cannot smell it.

In the dark, an octopus
uses its eight arms to feel for
food. It has grabbed a crab.

But moray eels are also out at
night. And they like to eat octopus!
The eel attacks. It bites the
octopus on one arm.

But the octopus can break
off its own arm! Now it is free.
It squirts out a cloud of dark ink.
This is its chance to escape.
*Whoooosh!* Off it goes!

At night, coral finds food. Out come its tentacles. The tentacles have poison stingers.

Back and forth they wave in the water. They trap tiny plants and animals floating by.

Then the sun rises. The coral tentacles go back inside the polyp. The colorful fish come out of hiding. Another day begins in the life of the reef.

Coral reefs have existed for
millions of years. They were around
even before dinosaurs.

But they are more than just
beautiful homes for fish and plants.
Reefs help protect the shore from
storms. They provide food and
medicines.

But coral reefs are in danger! And
the enemy is us.

*Boom!*

Sometimes fishermen use dynamite to kill many fish at once. The blast can destroy a coral reef.

Pollution on shore can harm coral reefs and the fish who live there.

Fertilizers help crops grow. But
fertilizers can seep into the ground
and wash out to sea. They, too, harm
coral reefs.

But perhaps the greatest danger to reefs is global warming.

Global warming means that the average temperature of the entire Earth is increasing.

Have you heard of greenhouse gases? They are natural gases in the atmosphere. They form a layer around our planet. Greenhouse gases help keep our planet nice and warm.

Just like the glass walls of a greenhouse, gases like carbon dioxide hold in heat from the sun.

But people have been adding more and more of these gases to the atmosphere.

How? We release these gases when
we drive cars . . .

We also release these gases when we use electricity, and when we heat or cool our homes.

The layer of greenhouse gases has

become too thick. Too much heat is trapped in the atmosphere.

This means the weather is warmer in many parts of our planet.

But what does global warming
have to do with coral reefs?
When the ocean is even a little bit
too warm, coral may bleach.

It turns ghostly gray or white.
Bleaching can be a sign that the
coral is about to die.

Scientists worry about the
coral reefs.

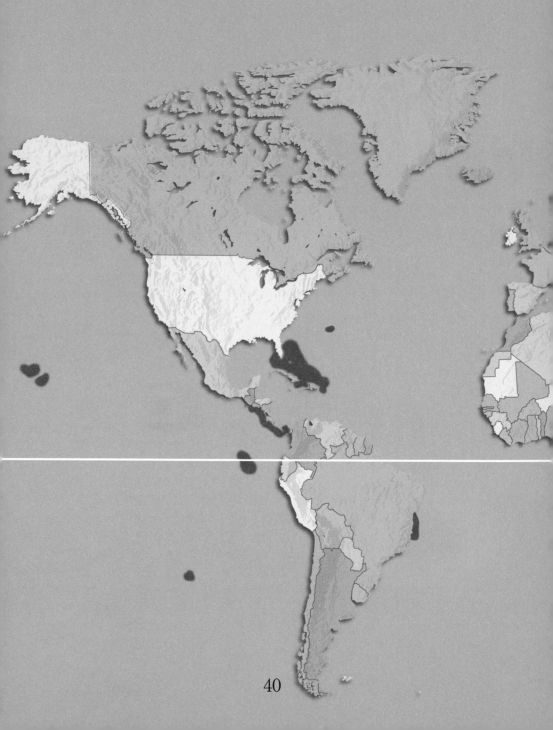

The green areas show coral reefs that are in danger. Up to one-third of the world's coral reefs have already died.

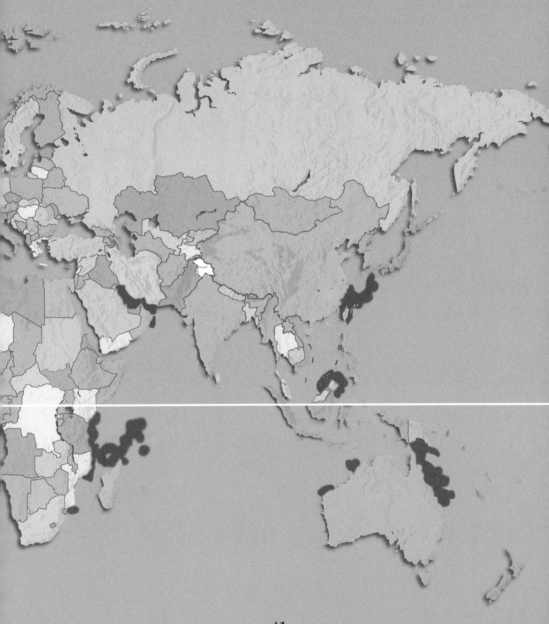

It is not too late to save coral
reefs. It is not too late to stop global
warming.

Here are some things you can
do to help.

Ask your family to walk or ride
bikes to places close by. Try to use
less electricity. Remember to turn off
lights.

In winter, use less fuel to heat your home. Wear a sweater indoors.

In summer, use less air-conditioning.

Open a window for a cool breeze.

Plant a tree! Trees remove carbon dioxide from the air. (Remember, carbon dioxide is one of the major greenhouse gases.)

Tree roots also hold on to soil.
They stop too much sediment
from getting into the ocean.
Sediment makes the water too
cloudy for coral to grow.

Coral reefs are truly one of the world's natural wonders. We must do our part to make sure that coral reefs will be around for millions of years to come.